A Declaration of A Body of Love
Poetry
By Lateef H. McLeod

Atahualpa Press
Houston, Texas 77072
atahualpapress66@yahoo.com

Library of Congress Control Number: 2008943445
McLeod, Lateef H. 2008
A Declaration of A Body of Love
1. Title

ISBN 0-9726483-3-X

Cover Photograph by Richard Downing © 2007

Printed in the United State of America
Atahualpa Press
Houston, Texas 77072

for my grandmother, Jenina Linton, who will be with me always

Table of Contents

I. Love of Disability

II. Love of the Stranger

III. Love of the Familiar

IV. Love of Culture

V. Love of the Theatrical

Love of Disability

Wall

This sharp clawing at the back
    of the neck
loneliness clutching my throat
I suffocate from the emptiness I
    feel alone and invisible
my friends and family
say they want to hang around
    me
I hear whispers of them in the
    breeze

I can't use my 3000 dollar light writer as a
    paperweight
a tortoise tries to crawl a race with a bullet
    train
the word-prediction capabilities
don't shield me from the impatient faces
that tap their toes

their eyes always wander looking for the
    next novelty
they need patience
but my cell phone goes deathly for hours in
    the day

can't we just find a fiber optic
        way
to hook my brain to the
        Machine
so my thoughts can be electronically voiced
over twelve-inch speakers

So we left with a clear wall
made of shards of ice and glass
I can see this barrier everyday
the sun glinting off its clear
        reflection
everyone acts as if it were not
        there
and does not see me cut my
        hand and feet
as I try to knock this wall down
I kick and punch until my feet
        and hands
are oozing with blood
I yell myself hoarse like a
        bullfrog
but I cannot get my family and
        friends to get close to me
so they really know

my dreams, thoughts, desires,
      and feelings
I shiver behind this clear wall
and wait for someone to notice
      me
wait for a chance to speak

The Silent Board

As a child
a piece of wood
with labeled pictures on it
was my voice
my vocabulary was limited
to words on a board

Words like
mommy
daddy
grandma
sister
cousin
eat
drink
bathroom
words and pictures
that encompass
my toddler life
without spaces
where I could
voice my mind

as I yearned to speak
those words beyond my board
My first Touch Talker
unlocked my words
I could now
type on the device
letter by letter
to say exactly what I wanted
and allow me to show
the brilliance of my mind
through my own voice

My voice is now limitless
words become notes
blaring building blocks
where I build my literary symphony
which echoes throughout the world

Absence of routine

Slender grey lines
on jacket sleeves
that musty smell on my clothes
drool is all over me
and you think it is disgusting

"Just swallow"
you say to me
and I really do try
catch and force down
pools of drool
from coming out of my mouth
cuz I be wearing tight fits
like Rocawear jeans, big Ekco
            shirts, Gap hoodies
or fresh to def in tailor-made suits
and drool does not go
with tailor-made suits
you know I try to look suave
            24/7
so at a party I can get my
            grown man on

So there shouldn't be a problem with
me swallowing, right?
Well I have to remember to
        swallow
every minute
every hour
every day

that means when I roll down the street
swallow
whenever I talk to someone
swallow
when I exercise
swallow
when I go to school
swallow
cuz I don't want anyone to see
        me drool, especially you
you always say that
it makes me look gross
and it is not my intention
to disgust you
so I try to swallow
like a mad man

I
(swallow)
try and
(swallow)
consciously do something
(swallow)
that everyone else
(swallow)
does unconsciously
(swallow)
and you still
(swallow)
can't understand
(swallow)
why
(swallow)
can't I
(swallow)
learn
(swallow)
to swallow all
(swallow)
the time
(swallow)

it is like
(swallow)
to toss you a tennis ball
(swallow)
telling you
(swallow)
to throw it
(swallow)
in the air and catch it
(swallow)
every 15 seconds
(swallow)
and yell at you
(swallow)
when you drop the ball
swallow just swallow
come on and swallow you know you want
        to

The pain of sitting

Secure in my walker
I take a sojourn around the
      block
my legs cramped
since I spent the three weeks in
      my wheelchair
the pre-atrophy of leg muscles
throbs at the back of my knees
as I start to walk
each step I take
I slow
 until I drag one foot
in front of other
a little tingle at first
then it grows to an itch
I cannot scratch
I can feel my
hamstrings
pull
itch
shorten
behind

my legs
and burn when I walk
I needed to stretch before
pain flows up my thighs
fire spreads from my toes to my
          butt
why didn't I walk yesterday
the day before yesterday

or even a week before that
do something to
stop my hamstring from
turning to a rigid rebar cement
          pole
so I cannot walk ever again

Strange encounters with the stupid kind

I just want to ask you a
        question
just one simple question
"What frat is that on your
        jacket?"
but when I roll up to you
and asked the question with my
        talker
you exclaim "get away from
        me" and abruptly walk away
now I know I don't look like an
        idiot
with my designer jeans and
        expensive Nike sneakers
and the talker I speak eloquently with
and create art out of syntax
        grammar structure
that your closed mind would not even
        fathom

and yet you walk away from a
        free lesson
of how to shatter your
        assumptions

a lesson I would freely teach
        you
and from the looks of it
your are in desperate need for
        the abridged course
but I understand if you have to
        go

nobody probably taught you
you stop and listen
when a wise man
decides to drop some knowledge in your
        lap

Better Things To Do

Oh no, it's me again
strolling down in my
      wheelchair
you don't want to talk to me
so you plot a course to avoid
      me
and I understand
really, I do
'cuz you have better things to
      do
going to Berkeley
and you don't have time to talk
      to me
especially since I have to type each word
      on my talker
and wheelchairs remind you of
      hospitals
and I drool
and only retards drool

so you walk away
fast as you can
wondering how I can get into
      UC Berkeley

23

and I wonder the same about
you

Power Soccer

With precision
I wield my Quickie P222
like a katana blade
and kick the soccer ball
down court
pass dumbfounded defender
who blink with amazement
as I pass them
and pass the ball to my teammate
who passes back to me
which leaves me open
to score a shot on goal
to the joyous cheers
of my teams and fans

You may look at me in my chair
and not believe my soccer skills
but get in a chair
and come try me on the court
your head will be spinning
about how fast I'll pass you
and score on you
but don't get mad
I told you I got game

Fortune

We just two C.P. Kids
in Kindergarten
in the "special day" class
our teacher
proud that she teaches a Kennedy daughter
does not recognize
what teaching two little black Cerebral
Palsy children can produce
two buckwheat children in her eyes
we can learn nothing
do nothing
are nothing
invisible

We are
kids with tennis bands on our wrists
bands to wipe our drool with
but we still think we are coo
especially you in your fat black pig tails
we do not worry about the people who look
        at us strange
even the children who tease us
who do not prepare us with thick enough

skin
to grow up as black people with cerebral
palsy
in 1986
I got my ticket
out of that "special day" class
out of that one way track to that "special
care" home
disabled prison

But what about you
you do not get to go to regular first grade
math class
and do regular arithmetic with other regular
children
as I do
you get stuck
with that same teacher
who stares at you through bifocals
and bangs away on her funky out-of-tune
piano
when she tries to teach you
she teaches you that you are ugly
instead of teaching you writing so you can
write an epic claiming your beauty
she teaches you that you are physically

27

inferior because you walk with a limp
instead of teaching you that your body is
     divine
and you should walk and exercise every
     day
teaches you that you are developmentally
slow because you drool
instead of teaching that you can do
anything that you want to if you put your
     mind to it
you are dying from thirst for knowledge in
a desert of "special class"
crying out for one drop of an idea

Coco

Oh Coco
I wish fortune had smiled on
        you
to shine on your black pig tails
held together with plastic pink
        bubbles
but sadly
fortune you never had
with parents who will not or
        cannot
encourage your growth and
        development
as my parents encourage me
teachers just like our Ms.
        Kennedy's token tutor
who do not care who you are
as long as you are still and
        quiet
just keep invisible as Ralph
        Ellison
and people will discard you like used
plastic bags
lying in the filth in the gutter
such is your fortune, Coco

a black disabled woman

That fortune glares me in the
        face today
as I open this computer file
look at the picture my friend
        sends me
I do not recognize you at first
your face rough as a man
I am shocked to see bare
        breasts
which declare your femininity
naked and discarded as you are
my mind races to the inevitable
        conclusion
homeless woman
but then I notice your hand
your crooked CP hand
        resembles my own
forces a look in your eyes
clouded over in a gaze
that has seen too much horror
        to resemble
the child I once knew
recognition is a lethal injection
        to my heart

If you see a disabled black
man

If you see a disabled black man
in a chair on a Wednesday
near the clubs' table
in the middle of Sproul Plaza
on the UC Berkeley campus

hair long and braided
beard full of spit
a tattered Cal jacket
makes you weary of him
as he appears to be a bum from
        Telegraph
whom you must avoid
as he tries to talk with you
points with his gnarled fingers
to letters on his communication
        board
a piece of plastic
with letters and numbers on it

That he points with great
        intensity

with his hand waving in the air
and his fingers extended
spelling out his life woes
letter by letter
while you stand over him
the body odor and drool
wafts in your nose
compels you to leave him
even though it will be rude

If you see him roll
through the hundreds of people
who erode the concrete on
          Sproul Plaza
as he approaches you
will you not turn away but offer

Hello, how are you?

Love of the Stranger

Raining on an Oakland girl's parade

For this Oakland girl
it's not fair
all she wants
is to watch her school
Oakland Tech beat Berkeley
    high
watch the boys from the school
    play
in their dashing football
    uniforms
but you wannabe gangstas won't let her
you with your talk of gun
    clapping
cancel her school's game
a monsoon on her parade
the neighborhoods over the
    Contra Costa hills
say "What a poor girl in an
    unfortunate
      circumstance"
as they drive their BMW,
    Mercedes Benz or Lexus

to their own high school football game in
        Acalanes

but they fail to realize
you never stop raining on this
        girl's parade
since before she can remember
she's had to duck away from
        dingy alleyways where
you sell drugs
do drive bys

 jack innocent pedestrians
her mom doesn't let her hang
        out with her friends
in her own neighborhood
cuz she just might meet up with
        you
and the one place she thought
        she was safe
her school
you decide to stage a mini riot
and turn a place of education into a
battlefield
in your stupid mini war

36

but I guess you are so tough
you have to hide behind children to do your
        business

Three suspicious doctors

What is so threatening about
      three doctors?
doctors are supposed so save
      lives and make you feel
        safe
you should feel safe around
      doctors, I thought
then why in Miami, Florida, did
      they think they are a
        threat?
      why did the Miami police arrest
      these three doctors?
did other Americans have to
      fear them?
did they look the way a terrorist
      should look?
are we to fear every Muslim
      man in the United States?
the people in Miami will say
      yes
as they put these three doctors
two of them American citizens
in jail for a "terror scare"

since a patriotic American
        woman heard them
say something suspicious
making her do her patriotic
        duty by calling the police
on everyone that looks brown
        and foreign
so they were arrested
banned from Larkin
        Community Hospital
where these doctors were doing
        their residency
their U.S. Citizenry was
        declined
to keep Americans safe from
        people who pray five
            times a day

Yellow Journalism

"Slum priest"
you actually
have the gall
to call
him
a
slum
priest

Excuse Me

Is this
the same priest
you championed
in '94
as the priest of the poor
the rightful leader of Haiti
you call now a slum priest

A decade ago
your articles herald
Clinton's replacing
the Papa Doc regime

The
rightful
elected
president
of Haiti
Aristide

But now
the end of his
second term is
too long for him
to remain in office

You imply
that he's no better
than a ruthless dictator
like a Saddam
or a Mobutu

But I
can see through lies
like a see-through shower curtain
to your ugly ass
              truth

I know
you don't care
who controls Haiti
as long as they stay
poor
hungry
depressed
angry
so that the next time they rebel
you can write another
"award-winning" news story

Well listen
the next time
you want to
exploit

third-world black countries
and discredit a good man's
        name
as good journalism
you won't have to wait until
Mr. Jayson Blair burns your
        house down

because believe me
I will

Last summer in New Orleans

Death hovers over me
       constantly
wind swept my house away
and now I am alone, wet and
       cold in this pool of waste
a lake of debris I wade in with a
       stench so foul
that my eyes water and I gag
       constantly
I hold onto tree as water rushes
       under me
wind tries to knock me over
I have only the clothes on my
       back
I hold on to that tree for one
       day
two days
three days
four days
no food or water to nourish my
       body
thirst produces salty drool and a
       white circle around my
          lips

finally the fifth day the paramedics pick me
    up in a helicopter

they carry me up from the tree
    that has been my home
for the last five days
as I am reeled in the wind
    blows me sideways I feel
as I am falling
as I fall gravity squeezes my
    loins
I melt in the paramedics arms
    as they carry me to
    Houston
from the helicopter I see electrical flames
    consume cars whole

the flames a painful light
    dancing to an unknown
      beat
my city is under water and
    burning at the same time
I arrive at the Houston arena
I can finally eat, drink, and
    shower

I never believed that hot water
       on my body could be so
       soothing
I shower myself with a
       hydraulic explosion
and cry over my lost city

My eyes look like a hundred
       feet kicked dirt in my
       face
my city that bury roots deep in
       history
I think of the history lost
my people's history
the beautiful African and
       Creole history
lost forever in the Gulf Coast
New Orleans used to be filled
       with the sound of jazz
hot rhythms make bodies whine
       to the big sound of the
       Big Easy
but not now, now my city is an
       abandoned ghost town
and I am a refugee in my own
       country

The Infectious Beat

I can hear the beat
beat of drums
enduring barrages
from calloused hands
boom baba boom bababa boom
a heart beat of my people
this constant thumping
kept their life force flowing
ba boom boom baba boom
from West Africa
the Mandinka used to say:
"in the beginning there was the
        drum"
and at least for West Africans
it was true
because it was the beat
this boom boom ba boom
that allowed the griots
to keep volumes
of their people's history
so they can be walking libraries
for their people to research
        from

it was the beat
the boom ba boom boom
that allowed my ancestors
to endure
when the white man
kidnapped them from their
       home
brought them across the
       Atlantic Ocean
in rickety wooden slave ships
to enslave them
taking away
their names
their language
their history
all they had left was the beat
that ba boom boom ba boom
cuz the beat was with them
on those slave ships
on those auction blocks
in those sugar cane fields
the beat is the spirituals
that they sung

to keep their eyes on heaven
when their lives were hell
freedom for my ancestors
meant freedom for the beat
yeah that boom ba boom boom
from Blues to Calypso
to Ska to Samba
to Gospel to Jazz
to Salsa, to Rhythm and Blues
to Reggae, to Soul,
to Funk, To Dancehall
to Soca, To Hip Hop
and it don't stop
that boom scratch boom boom
the beat lives on
in my people
and other people
whether you are
Irish or English
Indian or Pakistani
Japanese or Korean
Hutu or Tutsi
American or Iraqi
you know you want to
get down to the beat

so dance and enjoy yourselves
because you look ridiculous
when you stare at each other
and tap to the beat
boom boom scratch boom
       boom break

Love of the Familiar

My Protest Poem

This is my poem
against the doctors
who told my parents
I never would walk
or comprehend what I was
      saying to them
I should walk over to these
      doctors in my walker
and spit this poem at them

This poem is for the kids in my
      neighborhood
who teased me because
I was in a wheelchair
I used a device to speak
I drooled more than I
      swallowed
to them I was supposed to be
in a special day class
not share their dream
      of college
of middle class America

I was their pity case
I want to flash my
UC Berkeley graduation ring at
          them
and say "Who's the genius
          now"

This poem is for my roommate
my second freshman year of
          college

who was always drugged out
          on Ecstasy
he was the perfect
1600 SAT Score model
          American
who belonged in UC Berkeley
I was that gullible, black,
          cripple student
he could freeload off of
get free room and board
for absolutely nothing
except to put me to bed
that conflicted with his
appointments at raves
he was kicked out of school

I succeeded in fulfilling my
      dreams
leaving him in the dust
tasting the sweet honey nectar
      of revenge

Most importantly this poem is
      for Mark
who was my attendant
he memorized
every single of my four digit
      ATM pin
so he could steal 60, 80, 150
300 dollars from my checking
      account
who physically and verbally
      abused me
made fun of me when I drooled
severed our relationship like the
butcher knife he threatened me
      with
in my own home
who lied to me
countless times
that he was my friend
that I could trust him

55

that he had my best interest at
        heart
I want to beat him to a pulp
but I know all that will be for
        nothing
so I silently forgive all these
        hypocrites
and I try to love them again

Hole

I am missing something
something important
something that makes me
who I am
I remember people saying that I
      have a happy disposition
that I make other people's day just by
smiling and being with
      them
I seem to miss that part of
      myself
as if it has been hiding
I can't name it
but I feel its vacancy
like a big hole in my heart
this gape in my soul makes my
      body shiver
love has left me
and that makes God shake my
      head in disapproval
Mark didn't take it away though
I drove it out with my hatred of
      him

I allowed my pain
to control my thought and
          actions
for a year
I became what I hated
I abused my attendants
I ran one of them down in my
          wheelchair
and called another one
a woman mind you
ignorant and annoying
I have become another Mark
and the only thing I can do to
          reclaim me
is to let love back in
I need to forgive him
I need to forgive Mark
to forgive him for all the lies
the constant teasing
the derogation
the molestation
the stealing
I need to forget all the things he
          did to me
and love him as a person

and pray all this anger out of
     my heart
that began to rot my insides
then I can reclaim myself and
     be made whole

A mother's love

I know you love me
I know you would do anything
        for me
sacrifice anything for me
even your life

I know you spend
a good portion of
each day
just worrying about me
hoping that I am alright

So you call me
almost every day
call my attendants
almost every day
call half the people I know
almost every day

And I have to admit
at first I was slightly annoyed
thought it better if you backed

let me handle things and be a
     man

But you saw what I didn't see
how I needed you
your love and constant
     counseling
to help me through my
     challenging life

You once told me
you took over twelve hours
to give birth to me
twelve hours to give birth
but something went terribly
     wrong in labor
I didn't get much air at that
     critical time
the result
the challenge
to deal with the diagnosis
of cerebral palsy for the rest
     of my life

You vowed that day
of my birth
to love me with all your heart
to take care of me with all your
          strength
to make sure I was always safe
and you always did

With all my rebelliousness
and lack of tolerance
I slowly pushed you away
my heart became stone
yours broke into pieces

I should
pick up the pieces of your heart
put them back together
and stay in the bosom of your
          heart
forever

Grandma

Grandma, I got to tell you I
      love you
got tell you that you're so
      precious
that all the emeralds and the
      diamonds
are specks of dust compared to
      you
Grandma, I got tell you how
      much you mean to me
to help me from a boy to a man
you did so much you were like
      a super hero
with your bright red cape with a
      big gold G on it
it was you who cooked
cheesy spinach lasagna and
      spicy, hot jerk chicken
you who woke me up and
got me ready for school each
      morning
struggling with me to
get me out of bed

put on my clothes and feed me
before the bus came
you who took me
to therapy appointments
and you nodded off to sleep
as I tried to make you read
      stories
while the therapists worked on
      me
you were tired
tired from cleaning our house
day in and day out
tired from washing our clothes
tired from making our beds
tired from taking care of me
and my two sisters
and sometimes my legions of
      cousins
but you still did it
until the stroke stopped you
now you cannot speak
do not have to speak
as I lay my head on your
      shoulder

wishing that I could take care
       of you
as you took care of me

No more Teefy-boo

The nick name
"Teefy-boo"
out of my grandmother's mouth
used to make
dimples appear
on my face
as smiled in her arms
smelled her rich perfume
as she held me tight

The name had a secret meaning
of the special grandson
who couldn't do no wrong
didn't get whooped
when all the rest of
my sisters and cousins did
even if I instigated the trouble
        making
in the first place
and when she cooked
all those home cooked
        Jamaican meals
and her signature cheesy
        spinach lasagna

66

I knew it was especially for me
That is why
after her stroke
that took her speech
and her ambulatory ability
I prayed for her to be healed
and when I watch her health
        deteriorate
and she had to go in and out of
        the hospital
like it had a revolving door
I got on my knees and prayed
        for her to come home
and when she went into the
        hospital the last time
and laid in the I.C.U. with a
        tube up her nose
I wrung my hands together and
        prayed to see her smile
and when my whole family
went to her funeral and burial
I only cried
Now the utterance of the name
        Teefy-boo

only means
that I cringe
and force back tears

God's Gift

I praise you Oh Lord
with shouts and praises
I will offer
my body
my mind
my soul
to serve You
the ultimate Author
of my life

Every day
without fail
You wake me up
and send me on my way
with blessing and guidance
priceless gifts I cannot repay

Your Love is endless
patiently You watch
and shake Your head
as I still
lust after girls
worry about my future
get angry when people stare at me

you are still faithful

You blessed me
with a way with words
to string them as a melody
to delight people's ears
With the harmony of my literary voice

I will use my talent to your glory
and let my words warm the hearts of all
who read them
and when they want to give me all the
          praise
I will tell them that you should get all the
          honor instead

Valentine Flowers

These flowers I give
of vibrant red, orange and
        violet
are but a token
of gratitude
for you
who give time
to listen to me
in church
where I feel lucky
every time I get a chance
to sit next to you
you always radiant and elegant
with your designer shoes and
        Gucci scarves

Or on the phone
where I can spend hours
just to tell you all
my trials and tribulations
and you listen and give me
        encouragement
your mere voice gives me

strength to face all my
      challenges

Or on an outing to
the movies
a restaurant
a basketball game

where we can make each other
      laugh
sometimes by looking at each
      other
your light green eyes
pierce my brain as if you can
      see my exact thoughts

You have patience
as I talk to you
with synthesized speech
from my state-of-the-art
Dynawrite communication
      device
that barley substitutes
for my regular voice
that only can stammer out
hi and bye

at the beginning and end
of phone conversations

I got to give thanks to you
for being there for me
especially when my grandma
            died
we went out that Saturday
my tears turn to laughter
as we hit up the M.O.A.D.
            museum
and the new bougie Frisco mall
and you always have to
exclaim with delight
every time we pass a new
designer shoe display
You even went to my
            grandma's funeral
your mere presence helped heal
my heart's gaping wounds
and even though you did not
meet this woman
who loved me and raised me
with her heroine ability

and made me feel the presence
        of her love
every time I was with her
I know that if she had met you
she would have thanked you
for continuing part of her
        legacy
to make her favorite grandson
smile

A Valentine's Phone Conversation

Your voice
rich with melody
caresses my ears
with notes of tenderness
echoes through
my bluetooth earpiece
as I wish
that at least
I could feel
the breath
with those words
from your mouth
with luscious lips
as you tell me
about your day

But all I have is this earpiece
and this Iphone
which is cool
but as I talk
I want to hold your hand
look in your eyes
smell your perfume
as we hug

but I will settle
to hear you laugh
as I tell an ingenious joke

Let me laugh with you
though a chasm
of more than a thousand miles
that separate us
let's talk about each of our bible studies
of your choir practice
of my soccer practice
revel in the joy
to slowly discover each other
until the day
arms enclose shoulders
in love

A Rolling Love

You say you can't love me since I can't
     walk by your side

say you can't love me
since I can't walk by your side
but you can sit on my lap and we can
     roll around with pride

You say you can't love me since I can't
smooth talk you
     through the night
say you can't love me
since I can't smooth talk you
     through the night
but with my talker, baby
I can say the words to woo you
     Right

You say you can't dance with
     me
since I roll over your feet

say you can't dance with me since I roll
        over your feet
but, baby if we are together
every night we will grind to the beat

Dating Blues

No woman for me, no they are
      not for me
no fine lady for me, no they are
      not for me
I can't seem to find a woman
      for me

Call a woman up and she hangs
      up
try to holla at this woman and
      she hangs up
I guess I can't talk to her
      because she is stuck up

Call this other lady to start
      something good
said called this other Nubian
      queen to start something
      good
said she is talking to my frat
      brother and that is not
      good

I need only one woman to

cherish and call my own
yeah just need only one lady to
cherish and call my own
if I don't have a lady in my life
what's the point of being
grown

This woman must be dark with
a lot of curves
my special woman must be
dark with a lot of curves
a pale skinny woman will just
get on my nerves

Your Mama Don't Like Me

Your mama put a hex on me every time I
    go over there
I said my your mama put a hex
    on me
    every time I come over there
last time she made me loose my
    mojo honey
    and that ain't fair

Your mama really hates me
    honey
    as far as I can see
said your mama hates me
    honey
    as far as I can see
she likes to bring her pit bull and order it to
    jump me

Your mama shouts and cusses at me every
    day
your mama shouts and cusses
    at me every single day

with all those shouts and cusses I don't
    know how I can stay

Said the one that keeps me here is that I'm
    in love with you

only thing that keeps me here baby is that
    I'm so in love with you

but you keep siding with your
    mama baby and that just ain't coo

Sonnet For F.D.G.

You who could have chosen any man chose
      me
a man who longed for a woman like you
after years of searching for one I couldn't
      see
you appeared a welcomed sight in my view
from a far you encouraged me the chase
enticing me with your smile to be yours
and even with my promise to be now chaste
you promise sexual passion is ours
now I wait for the day and the exact time
when I can lay with you and hold your
      body
and feel your heart beat synchronize with
      mine
let's rock the bed make noise and be rowdy
every second and minute of our time
I am glad you decided to be mine

Love poem for S. H.

She whispers secrets in my ear
her breath swirls and tickles my
       ear drums
every murmur turns to a
       melody
that hypnotizes me
like a snake does a charmer
I am helplessly
drawn to her

There those brown eyes that
       penetrate me
jet black hair that smells like
       Head & Shoulders
she wears it in a hair wrap far
       too often
her olive skin still radiates
showing under her all white
       outfits

When I am privileged to talk to
       her
I am turned into that reckless
       third grader

who told everyone I liked Erica
    Smedbloom
the kids teasing made her cry

This woman with eyes like
    daggers

and a smile of sure brilliance
is no child
she is in the NBA
and I'm playing
high school ball

When I first saw her
she was a Def Poet
who told her story to the world
with a voice loud and defiant
like a true Brooklynite
the spotlight made her shine
    brightly on stage
and I fell in love with her words

Now she teaches me
that I have the same power
with words as she does

to ignite the fire in people's
        hearts
as she did in mine

I will not tell her I dream about
        her
or that she is my muse
and a flood of poems rush in
        my head
every time I think about her
but what I will tell her
I need to hear her voice again
I need to see her eyes boring
        into me again

I need to feel her touch on my
        skin
and that will be enough
for now

The Amazing Adventures of
Fred and Teef

Fred and I are quite the same
young, black, men
with our lives in front of us
we feel we can do anything we
       want
and we mostly do
partners in crime
we go out on the town
in our dapper suits
and we can't help if
five women follow us home
we just got it like that
and of course we are jet setters
we travel to
Los Angeles
Las Vegas
Charlotte, North Carolina
St. Louis
and wherever we go
people say we shine like
       diamonds

but we pay them no mind
we are too busy
strutting on the dance floor
floating like butterflies
and we are so pretty
even Muhammad Ali will get
        jealous
now people might ask Fred if I
        slow him down

being in a wheelchair
but he probably say
"Lateef is the one partying all
        night tiring me out"
and he is right

A Visit

My friend
hooked up to
a respirator
and arms strapped
to a hospital bed
still has enough strength
to grip my hand
and do our handshake
which ends with him
snapping his fingers
that echoes in the hospital room
In a hospital room
not hanging out
at my crib
listening to
the new David Banner
"Get Like Me"
or on the sticks
playing NBA Live '08
on his new Xbox 360
or at a Warrior game
with me clowning
that they beat the Spurs

again
or at a club
where we peep
all the baddest ladies
and take turns
showing off our tightest moves
just laughing
far away
from here
In this hospital room
from a bullet
shot from a gun
whose trigger
a total fool pulled
who has no idea
how much you mean to me

Love of Culture

Just Chillin'

Just chillin' on a sultry summer
       night in Florida
I watch my dad and my uncles
       play domino
Jamaican style domino of
       course
a classic game of take six
I learn something
without being taught something

My Uncle Ned
boasts he is the best player
he bangs a certain domino on
       the table
and causes all the dominoes to
       fly
to skip the player next to him,
block the game,
or win the game
five in a row and
blurts out "Come test me" like
       he planned all of this

his opponents
wonder which is worse
to get beat by him or
hear him brag

My dad and Uncle Ian say
"I just match numbers"
they win the next four games
with Uncle Ian taking a tally

  after every game
"1…that's 2…3 now…See here
  is 4"
to postpone but not defeat
Uncle Ned and Uncle Sadiq's
  six game
win of the series

But all of them were happy
someone is marrying their niece
a niece with four children
children who now have a father
making my aunt, the bride's
  mother, happy
making my father and uncles
  happy

so this night they will laugh
and after the wedding I see
      these
macho Jamaican men cry tears
      of joy

The Quintessential Yardie

To my Jamaican family

Me a Yardie for true
and like all yardies Jamaica's
        my home
and my home resembles
        paradise
with beach sand
whiter than pearl
contrasting the ocean
blue as sapphire
but I can't live there
'cuz the IMF jacked my country
and now it's so deep in debt
no one can get jobs
so gunmen lay stick up kid
to feed their pickni' em
and shoot up the whole place
so us Yardies stay away
in Flatbush, Brooklyn
in Miami, Florida
in Toronto, Canada
in the Bay

'cuz anywhere Yardies are
my home is also
and we all eat ackee and drink
      sorrel
listen to the latest riddim
waiting for Ja to be irie and
      safe

Stop sittin on you bombo

Me think you big man
Cal graduate
got your Master's from Mills
Mista Toppa Top
yes sah
but look at you got no job
no money
no bling-bling
wa wrong wit you bwai?
don't you know?
all you friend dem have jobs
you sister have job
and you just sit a yard watch
        CNN
you mad?
think a job come bump you
        head
you worthless bwai
mus work to look fi job, seen
and cerebral palsy a no excuse
plenty big C.P. toppa tops in
        town

wa you waiting for?
you Big Teef from yard?
aim fi you job then
and bruk it out of di sky

Love of the Theatrical

Procrastination: My age old friend

Yo Procrastination
what man
can't you see I'm getting some
shut eye
we need to reconsider our
friendship
because as it appears now
you want me to fail
hey you got me all wrong
you actually want me to
miss all my deadlines
and be late to all my
appointments
no I only remind you of the
things
that you want to do
it is not my fault you have extra
duties
you should be doing
you actually get a kick out of it
to watch me hurry up

to write
a poem or a paper
in a day and a half
when I had two weeks to do it
it is a crack-up to watch you
hunched over the computer
sweat pouring down your face
and where did those two weeks
go?

was it sucked up in
an inter-dimensional vortex?
no it was when I listen to you
me?
to go to this party
to hang with these friends
to go to this movie
to read this novel
instead of studying
got me into this mess
so this is my fault now?
like you are blameless
yeah right
and you are no-where to be
found

when I try to straighten out
this mess we made together
that is really not my scene
I had to spend time
with my shorty anyway
which just proves my point
       exactly
so for now on
I am not messing with you
yo I thought we were boys bruh
nah, bruh you are bringing me
       down
I will just go and start hanging
       out
with Punctual and Organized
because they understand I have
       business to take care of
have fun with those losers

Punctual goes to a party thirty
       minutes

before the party starts
and leaves before the honeys
arrive and it cracks

then Organized does not even
          go out
cuz he is always busy
getting his house in order
if you hang out with those two
you will have no life

well at least my nonexistent life
will be successful
cuz really bruh
I see no fun
to see every opportunity
pass me by
cuz I wait too late
to act on it

Life With Mark (a stage act)

Scene 1

I trusted you with my body
with my very life
you were my number one guy
you trusted me with your
        secrets
remember all those secrets
secrets you didn't tell your wife
I still remember them
but they won't leave my lips
and I won't write them down for everyone
to see
I am not deliberately vindictive
like you
your face is stone
 rock hard stone
indispensable even by my smile
rigid like granite
I can feel your anger radiating
        off you
and it burns me like you were
        nuclear toxic waste

must I have to wear nuclear
        protective gear when
dealing with you
every cold stare and cold
        shoulder
every act of passive aggression, each time
you purposely
        mishandled me
slamming me hard on the toilet bruising my
buttocks
and the silence

the absolute silence between
        you and me
I can't take when it slowly
        chokes me
my pharynx shrinks with every
        minute
I can't breathe
why do you stare at me with
        such disgust?
What did I do? What did I say? Did I hurt
you? Did I make you
        mad?
I apologize, please forgive me

I am sorry, so sorry, I won't do
        it again
I was wrong you are right
you are always right
so sorry so sorry so sorry so
        sorry
just please talk to me

Scene 2

Maybe I am a little too hard on
        you
yes, maybe I don't understand
        your story
I mean you came along way
from picking up those tennis
        balls
for those American tourists on
        those tennis courts
how impressionable then
 a young Filipino boy without

        any shoes
seeing how flashy dressed
those Americans were

108

you must have thought they had
        everything
or at least everything you ever
        wanted
you must have started dreaming
        about having everything as well
in your mind if you just could
        get to America your
                dreams can come true
as you grow older your desire
        to sojourn to America
                only intensifies
but you find that you need
        money and an American
                Visa to go
you start a cab company
see you already have that
        entrepreneurial spirit
you hope your business will
        hopefully give you
enough money for your
        travel
but you realize that money is
        hard to come by
how are you going to get to
        America?

then like an answered prayer she slips in
the taxi one
          day
a head manager of a large bakery chain
with stores in the US

you see your chance ad you go
          for it
so what if she is twenty years
          older than you
you marry her anyway
a perfect couple as far as you
          are concerned
and you slowly coax her to take
          visits to America
you get Visas in a flash
first visit a few weeks
second visit a few months
by the third visit you convince
          her to move there
you sly little devil you
and what better place then Daly
          City, California
at least there is a large Filipino
          population there

even though the temperature
stays just above 60 the whole
        year
no more tropical weather for
        you
but you are in America where
        all your dreams will
            come true
now all you need is a job
first you work at a bakery
but they don't pay enough
then you peep what your wife is
        doing part time
home health care
and it hits you like a lighting
        bolt
you can help take care of an
        elderly or a disabled
person and make some
decent dough
then your lovely wife introduced you to me
and this is where our story
        begins
isn't it?

Scene 3

You did think you could handle
      me
didn't you?
I was a young twenty-one year
      old college student
a Jamaican-American boy, new
      to the world
not a harden Filipino wiseass
from the cruel streets of Manila
you were familiar
to the concept of everyone out
      for himself
and you were not going to give
      up on that concept just
because you met me
you were friendly to me all
      right
a lovable bowl of laughs
but deep down you knew that
you could never be my true
      friend
to you I was a rich, spoiled
      American

It didn't matter that I was
       disabled
my struggles were not nearly as
       bad as yours
I have my parents there to
       support me
while you had to fend for
       yourself
I guess that is why you thought
I didn't mind
when you withdrew a couple
       hundred dollars from my
banking account a few
       times
you were going to put the
       money back eventually
really you thought I wouldn't
       miss it plus you had
some gambling debts and
other debts to pay off and
you needed fast cash
when you were fired the first
       time you realized I was
not the easy mark as you
       supposed

but when you were hired back
you realized also that I needed
        you more then you

            needed me
and that was too much power
        then you needed to have
you played your position
        perfectly
everyone we met
from my friends to my family
always said you were the
        perfect attendant
so attentive and well
            mannered
but when we were alone
you always made it clear who
            was boss
even though you called me boss
        anyway just for looks
living with you was like living
        with Jackal and Hyde
I never knew what attendant I
        would get in the morning

Scene 4

I am missing something something
important
something that makes me who
     I am
I remember people saying that I
     have a happy disposition
that I make other people's day just by
smiling and being with
     them
I seem to miss that part of
     myself as if it is been
      hiding
I can't name it but I feel its
     vacancy like a big whole
     in my heart
     wait that is it, love has left me
Mark didn't take it away though
I drove it out with my hatred of
     him
I allowed my pain to control
my thought and actions for a
     year

I became what I hated
I abused my attendants
I ran one of them down in my
        wheelchair
and called another one
a woman mind you
ignorant and annoying
I have become another Mark
and the only thing I can do to
reclaim me is to let love back in
I need to forgive him
I need to forgive Mark
I need to forget all the things
he did to me and love him
as a person
Then I can reclaim myself
and be made whole

Your Hands

In your hands
I surrender my body
to allow you to undress me
take off every article
of clothes
like when you peel a ripe orange
that you desperately want to suck
juices from

I know it is your job
to guide my body to the shower
where you scrub every inch of my body
clean
but the hair on my arms stand erect and
tingle
when your hand slightly brushes the muscle
of my arms and chest
your eyes relishes the sight
of little beads of water
that drips from my wet body

You are the one
to tell me

117

I look sexy
and describe my leg hairs
as a path to the secret garden
that you want to frolic in

I fall in love with the way you see me
not as a person with a weak cerebral palsy
body
but a sexy man with arm and chest muscles
you want to rub as you hold me
you hands etches the outline of my arms
and chest
your arms embraces my torso

But I know it is wrong
a sin so sweet that it leaves a cavity in our
soul
a dull pain after our bodies unraveled
the forbidden love between an attendant
and client
to know we broke our professional code
we feel the shame
as the blood from the hands of our Lord
and Christ
covers the spectacle
of how we lay naked on my sheets

Guilt tears us apart
but I remember how you saw me
how you accepted me as your man
and my heart rejoices
that your heart once desired mine
as I wait for another woman
to share your conviction
that I can be her man

My Secret Nude Ball

What a beautiful night for a celebration
I thank you for joining me on this
tremendous occasion
what are we celebrating you asked?
why none other than the end of my care
of what you think and preconceive
my body is and can do
cuz I know the truth
that I am a beauty to be hold
make perfect in the sight of God
You see that I dressed up for the occasion
with my white gloves
black cane and top hat
and of course
my snuggly fit flesh thong
that keeps my tender, endowed groin in
place

don't I look dapper and elegant
while I sit in my birthday suit in my chair
do not look away
but either relish me or gawk at me with
your eyes

I already said I don't care how
you perceive me
so while you sit and stare
I am going to dance
cuz this is my party
and I plan to have fun
and shake my booty
to my favorite dance hall, hip hop, and
salsa jams
you can join in if you want
but if you don't
it doesn't matter to me
It is my party, remember

See how my muscles gleam in the
moonlight
you eyes trace over my slender figure
as I dance on stage
you once saw me as a drooling, weak
invalid
admit it, you did
but now that you see me here
as I dance onstage
you can't deny that your eyes are locked on
to me
and you can't turn away

121

and even if you form arguments to disagree
-you and I know the truth is undeniable to
you
I am beautiful

A Declaration of A Body of
Love

Undressing myself is a special
      thing for me
because I do not normally do it
it is other hands that take off
my shoes
braces
socks
pants
jacket
sweater
shirt
     and chair
until I am left
naked
before them
so these foreign hands
not my own
can bathe me
scrub every inch of my body
     clean
so my shower turn into someone else's duty
a act to be checked off
my shower can never be a place

where I can claim privacy with
    my body

That's why some nights I get
    out of bed
undress in the moon light
I would only wear
a shirt and pajama bottoms
I pull my arm of one sleeve
then pull it over my head
then off my other arm
and let it drop to the floor
I flex my bare chest muscles in
    the mirror
then I slowly pull my pajama
    bottoms over my hips
and crawl out of them
lay them in a pile with my shirt
and crawl to my mirror in my
    room
touch and rub every inch of my
    body
my thick dick erect in front of
    me
my body shudders in the wind

my hands rub the muscles of
        my inner thigh
and then move ever so slowly
        upward
only to feel that twinge of
        remorse
after I finish

You see jacking off seems to be
        a problem
at least for me
even before fanatic Christians
told me it was a sin
I still felt guilty after doing it
for some strange reason
as if God was shaking His head
        in disapproval
I used to think that doing it will
make bad things happen to me
like I blamed the stomach flu that made me
miss my
high school senior breakfast
just cuz I masturbated the day
        before
and I thought I could get more
        dates

if I stopped playing with myself
so since high school I have
         been on a futile endeavor
         to be abstinent
sometimes I can go for weeks
         without it
but after weeks wilt will power
I do it again
disappointed with myself and
         ashamed
I try to work
to be celibate again
celibate, which really means
         alone

All I want
is my lady
my wife
to hold me

and I want to hold
my wife
feel at home
in her arms
the best feeling ever
better than sex

I don't know though
cuz I never really experience
        that before
Yes, I had sex with a few
        women
but I never felt the close feeling
        of
needing to hold my wife so
        tight
that our two heart beats become
        one
to feel the light whisper in my
        ear
that tingles my eardrum and
        then
vibrates through my whole
        body
with the same warmth
that encases me
like her body wrapped around
        me
her legs circle my waist
her arms fold across my chest
her breasts against my back

her head lays on my shoulder
and I lay back on her
as I finally find home

About the Author

Lateef McLeod holds a BA in English from UC Berkeley and a MFA in Creative Writing from Mills College in his home city of Oakland, CA.   In 2006, he joined the Augmentative and Alternative Communication Rehabilitation Engineering Research Consortium on Communication Enhancements (AAC-RERC) Writers Brigade where he wrote technical articles about the AAC community.   In addition to technical writing, Lateef's poetry has appeared in anthologies, magazine articles and other publications.

Lateef McLeod served as key-note speaker at the 2007 Bubbly Ball, and was the plenary speaker at the AAC By The Bay Conference in 2007.

His artistic _expression also came to life on stage during the 2007 Sins Invalid , An Unshamed Claim to Beauty show where Lateef's poetic voice filled the air at the Brava Theater in San Francisco.

130

Lateef's contributions towards the field of technology are ongoing as he writes articles for the Assistive Technology Network. His expertise in communication and technology led to his current position as a consultant for Dynavox.

For presentations and more information, you may contact the author at: lmcleod337@yahoo.com